BIENVENUE
DANS LE MONDE MUSICAL D'ABC MELODY !

La collection CHANTE & DÉCOUVRE est un concept innovant et ludique qui propose des chansons originales, amusantes et rythmées pour faire découvrir les langues étrangères aux enfants de la maternelle jusqu'à la fin du primaire.

Avec CHANTE & DÉCOUVRE L'ANGLAIS, l'initiation à l'anglais se fait naturellement et sans effort.

Chaque chanson est présentée avec son texte et son lexique illustré pour mieux comprendre les paroles lors de l'écoute. L'enfant est ainsi mis en confiance et chantera facilement. À l'aide des versions instrumentales, on pourra créer sa propre chanson en changeant un mot pour un autre.

L'équipe d'ABC MELODY

1 / ALPHA RAP
2 / I PUT ON MY HAT
3 / LOOK AT THE SKY!
4 / WAKE UP, GET UP!
5 / WHAT DO YOU LIKE TODAY?
6 / GOOD MORNING!
7 / HOP ON A TRAIN!
8 / BLUE LIKE THE SEA
9 / WORLD ALPHABET
10 / WHERE IS THE COW?

CHANSONS BONUS :

11 / WHAT COLOUR IS IT?
12 / RED BIRD, YELLOW COW, JUMP!

13-24 / VERSIONS INSTRUMENTALES

1 / ALPHA RAP

A B C

D E F G

H I J K

L M N O

P Q R S T

U V W

X Y Z

2 / I PUT ON MY HAT

I put on my hat
I put on my shoes
I put on my shirt
I'm ready to move!

Move to the left!
Move to the right!

I put on my dress
I put on my shoes
I put on my gloves
I'm ready to move!

Move to the left!
Move to the right!

I put on my socks
I put on my shoes
I put on my pants
I'm ready to move!

Move to the left!
Move to the right!

I put on my skirt
I put on my shoes
I put on my coat
I'm ready to move!

Move to the left!
Move to the right!

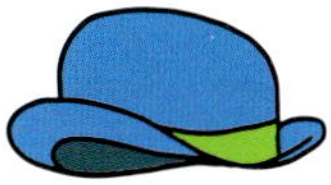

hat

shoes

shirt

dress

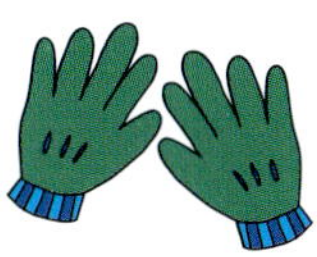

gloves

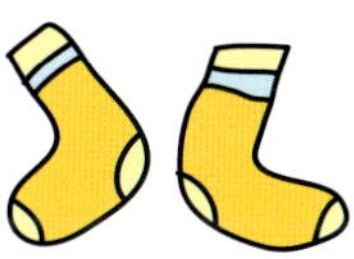

socks

pants / trousers

skirt

coat

left

right

3 / LOOK AT THE SKY!

Look at the sky!
The sun is shining.
Look at the sky!
The wind is blowing.
} x2

The weather is funny.
It's hot and sunny.
The weather is funny.
It's cold and windy.
} x2

Look at the sky!
Hey, it's raining.
Look at the sky!
Hey, it's snowing.
} x2

The weather is funny.
It's hot and sunny.
The weather is funny.
It's cold and windy.
} x2

The weather is funny... Yeeha!

to look

sky

sun

rain

snow

wind

The sun is shining.
It's sunny.

The wind is blowing.
It's windy.

It's hot.

It's cold.

It's raining.

It's snowing.

5 / WHAT DO YOU LIKE TODAY?

I like to play
I like to sing
I like to run
I like to swim

Hey hey hey!
What do you like to do?
Hey hey hey!
What do you like today?

I like my dog
I like my cat
I like my shoes
I like my hat

Hey hey hey...

I love my dad
I love my mum
I love my friends
They're so much fun!

Hey hey hey...

I like to play
I like to sing
I like to run
I like to swim

Hey hey hey...

Hey hey hey!
What do you like today?

I like / I love

I don't like

to play

to sing

to run

to swim

dog

cat

shoes

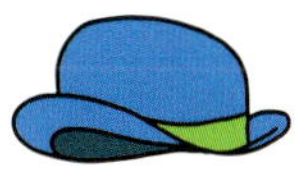

hat

Dad / father

Mum / mother

6 / GOOD MORNING!

Good morning,
good morning!
What's your name? } x2

My name is Jane
I'm a dancer
My name is Ben, oh, oh, oh
I'm a singer

Good afternoon,
good afternoon!
What's your name? } x2

My name is Fred
I'm a sailor
My name is Ted, oh, oh, oh
I'm a teacher

Good evening,
good evening!
What's your name? } x2

My name is Tim
I'm a baker
My name is Kim, oh, oh, oh
I'm a painter

Good night,
good night!
What's your name? } x2

My name is Jane
I'm a dancer
My name is Ben, oh, oh, oh
I'm a singer

Hey!
What's your name?

Good morning!

Good afternoon!

Good evening!

Good night!

My name is Jane.

My name is Ben.

dancer

singer

sailor

teacher

baker

painter

7 / HOP ON A TRAIN!

I'm going to school
Hop on a train!
I'm going to Spain
Catch a plane!

Hop on a train
Take the bus
Jump on your bike
Hop on a train
Take the bus
Jump on your bike
Come with us!

Hop on a tram
Catch a plane
Jump on a ship
Hop on a tram
Catch a plane
Jump on a ship
Count to ten
1, 2, 3, 4, 5,
6, 7, 8, 9, 10!

I'm going to school
Hop on a train!
I'm going to Spain
Catch a plane!

Hop on a train...

to go to school

to hop / to jump

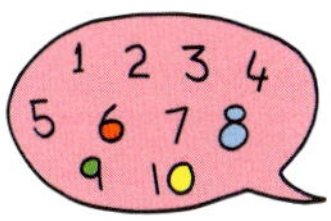

to count (to ten)

school

train

plane

bus

bike

tram

ship

8 / BLUE LIKE THE SEA

Blue, blue like the sea
Green, green like a tree
Red, red like a cherry
Brown, brown like a monkey

Yellow, yellow like a lemon
Pink, pink like a lolly
Orange, orange like a melon
White, white like a daisy

Black, black like the night
Grey, grey like a hippo
Purple, purple like my bike
Beautiful like a rainbow!

sea

night

tree

cherry

monkey

lemon

lolly / sweet

melon

daisy

hippo
(hippopotamus)

bike

rainbow

9 / WORLD ALPHABET

A	Australia
B	Brazil
C	China
D	Denmark
E	England
F	France
G	Germany
H	Honduras
I	India
J	Japan
K	Kenya
L	Latvia
M	Mali
N	Norway
O	Oman
P	Portugal
Q	Qatar
R	Russia
S	Spain
T	Togo
U	USA
V	Vietnam
W	Wales
X	?
Y	Yemen
Z	Zimbabwe

Australia

Brazil

China

Denmark

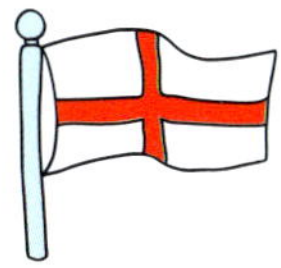

England

France

Germany

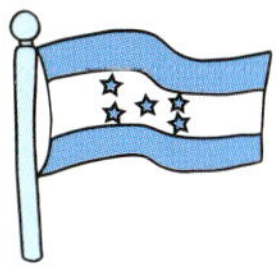

Honduras

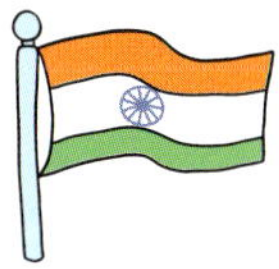

India

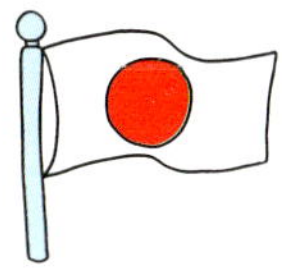

Japan

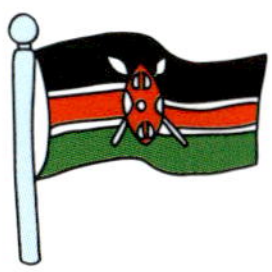

Kenya

Latvia

Mali

Norway

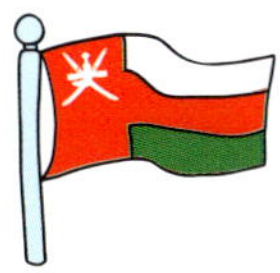

Oman

Portugal

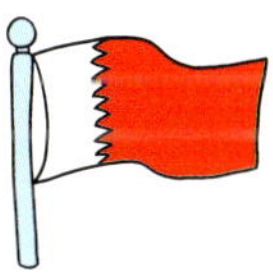

Qatar

Russia

Spain

Togo

USA

Vietnam

Wales

Yemen

Zimbabwe

10 / WHERE IS THE COW?

Where is the cow?
The cow is on the grass
Where is the mouse?
The mouse is in the house
Where is the sheep?
The sheep is in the shed
Where is the dog?
The dog is on the bed

Hello, hello!
We say hello
Welcome to the farm!
Welcome to the show!
} x2

Where is the horse?
The horse is in the stable
Where is the cat?
The cat is on the table
Where is the pig?
The pig is in the sty
Where is the bird?
The bird is in the sky

Hello, hello!
We say hello
Welcome to the farm!
Welcome to the show!
} x4

cow

mouse

sheep

dog

horse

cat

pig

bird

house

bed

grass

sky

Hello!

11 / WHAT COLOUR IS IT?

Blue, red, yellow,
What colour is it?
Is it blue? Is it red?
Is it yellow?
Blue, red, yellow.

Green, pink, brown,
What colour is it?
Is it green? Is it pink?
Is it brown?
Green, pink, brown.

Orange, purple, black,
What colour is it?
Is it orange? Is it purple?
Is it black?
Orange, purple, black.

12 / RED BIRD, YELLOW COW, JUMP!

Red bird, red bird, jump!
Yellow cow, yellow cow, jump!
Red bird, red bird,
Yellow cow, yellow cow,
Red bird, yellow cow, jump!

Green dog, green dog, jump!
Blue cat, blue cat, jump!
Green dog, green dog,
Blue cat, blue cat,
Green dog, blue cat, jump!

Black pig, black pig, jump!
White sheep, white sheep, jump!
Black pig, black pig,
White sheep, white sheep,
Black pig, white sheep, jump!

Pink mouse, pink mouse, jump!
Brown bee, brown bee, jump!
Pink mouse, pink mouse,
Brown bee, brown bee,
Pink mouse, brown bee, jump!

Pink mouse, pink mouse,
Brown bee, brown bee,
Pink mouse, brown bee, jump!
} x2